SETTLEMENT

Kidron Valley N. 31 46.404 E. 035 14.085 640 Metres West

Kidron Valley N. 31 46.404 E. 035 14.085 640 Metres North

MACK

SETTLEMENT

NICK WAPLINGTON

Kidron Valley N. 31 46.404 E. 035 14.085 640 Metres North East

Kidron Valley N. 31 46.404 E. 035 14.085 640 Metres East North East

Kidron Valley N. 31 46.404 E. 035 14.085 640 Metres East

Kidron Valley N. 31 46.404 E. 035 14.085 640 Metres South

This book's title refers to the Jewish communities built in the region of the former state of Palestine known as the West Bank, an area of approximately 5,628 square kilometres (2,173 square miles) between the Jordan River and Jerusalem, including the eastern sector of the city. This is the area that was administered by Jordan from 1948 to 1967, when it was occupied by Israel in the aftermath of the Six-Day War (the official annexation of East Jerusalem followed in 1980).

Israel's right to govern the West Bank is not recognised by the United Nations, which deems any Israeli building in this area to be a violation of international law. By contrast, the settlers refer to this territory as 'Judea and Samaria', designating it as the biblical land of Israel that was given to them by God 4,000 years ago. While all the settlers are Jewish, and almost all are Israeli citizens, many are not natives of Israel. Most of the men and women in these images are immigrants who arrived in the West Bank from the United States, South Africa, Australia, the United Kingdom, the former Soviet Union, and other parts of the wider Jewish diaspora.

The images in this book were created between 2008 and 2013, when I photographed over 350 distinct settlements, from populous cities like Ariel to tiny outposts made up of a few caravans. The exact number of settlements cannot be determined with accuracy, as both construction and demolition take place regularly throughout the region. In general, however, the presence of Jewish settlers in the West Bank is entrenched, and their building projects continue with the support of the state of Israel.

Beit Yonatan N. 31 46.404 E. 035 14.085 640 Metres East

East Jerusalem, view from Nof Zion settlement   N. 31 45.299 E. 035 14.546   714 Metres   East

Nof Zion N. 31 45.290 E. 035 14.543 760 Metres South South East

Nof Zion N. 31 45.290 E. 035 14.543 760 Metres South South East

Ramot N. 31 49.167 E. 035 11.722 793 Metres West South West

Jerusalem Light Railway Depot N. 31 48.530 E. 035 14.178 810 Metres East

Mitzpe Eshtemoa N. 31 23.451 E.035 00905 623 Metres North West

Gittit N. 32 06.189 E. 035 23.255 375 Metres East

Gittit N. 32 06.189 E. 035 23.255 375 Metres East

Psagot N. 31 54. 042 E. 035 13. 290 West

Beitar Illit N. 31 41 51 E. 35 06 56 North

Ibei Ha'Nahal N. 31 36.927 E. 035 13.309 783 Metres North East

Ibei Ha'Nahal N. 31 36.927 E. 035 13.309 783 Metres East

Shavei Shomron   N. 32. 15.016 E. 035 11.016   368 Metres   East

Towards Ma'ale Levona   N. 32 02.846 E. 035 15.694   733 Metres   West North West

View from Ma'ale Levona N. 32 03.320 E. 035. 14.559 780 Metres South East

Ma'ale Levona N. 32 03.320 E. 035 14. 560 783 Metres South East

Teqoa D N. 31 38.194 E. 035 14.668 577 Metres North

Gittit N. 32. 06.327 E. 035 23.472 378 Metres North

Teqoa A with Herodion   N. 31 38. 908 E. 035 13.818   674 Metres   North

WOLVES

Mishor Adumim Industrial Area N. 31 47.782 E. 035 20.488 246 Metres West

Mishor Adumim Industrial Area N. 31 47.782 E. 035 20.488 246 Metres North West

Mehola N. 32 21. 563 E. 035 30.081 235 Metres North East

Nofei Prat N. 31 49.143 E. 035 18.805 469 Metres East

Elon Moreh, view from Kabir Hill/Sultan's Tomb N. 32. 14.526 E. 035 19.685 765 Metres North

Elon Moreh, view from Settlement towards Kabir Hill / Sultan's Tomb N. 32. 13.968 E. 035 19.708 660 Metres North

Alon Road N. 31 50.199 E. 035 21.235 561 Metres South

Alon Road N. 31 50.199 E. 035 21.235 561 Metres South South West

Alon Road N. 31 50.199 E. 035 21.235 561 561 Metres West

Alon Road N. 31 50.199 E. 035 21.235 561 561 Metres South North West

Alon Road N. 31 50.199 E. 035 21.235 561 561 Metres North North West

Alon Road N. 31 50.199 E. 035 21.235 561 561 Metres North

Alon N. 31 49.919 E. 035 21.361 232 Metres North

Almog N. 31 47.241 E. 035 27.373 -231 Metres North East

Almog N. 31 47.241 E. 035 27.373 -231 Metres East

Qalya N. 32 45.084 E.035 27.824 -332 Metres South

Qalya N. 32 45.072 E.035 27.847 -334 Metres North

Ovnat N. 31 40.679 E. 035 26.182 -326 Metres North

Har Homa N. 31 44.107 E. 035 13.228 652 Metres South West

Har Homa N. 31 44.107 E. 035 13.228 652 Metres North West

Har Homa N. 31 44.107 E. 035 13.228 652 Metres North

Itamar   N. 32 09.985 E. 035 20.165   835 Metres   West

Beit Hagai N. 31 29.678 E. 035 04.704 839 Metres South East

Beit Hagai N. 31 29.678 E. 035 04.704 840 Metres North East

Metzad N. 31 35.090 E. 035 11.289 950 Metres East

Bethlehem from Har Homa N. 31. 43. 097 E. 035 13.228 653 Metres South West

Palestinian Farmland N. 31 59. 800 E. 035 06.092 344 Metres East

Hashmonaim N. 31 55.818 E. 035 01.442 235 Metres East South East

Halamish N. 32 005.02 E. 035 07.679 569 Metres North West

Halamish N. 32 005.02 E. 035 07.679 569 Metres South East

Har Adar N. 31 49.380 E. 035 07.491 856 Metres North

SPORT

Agan Ha'ayalot N. 31 51.763 E. 035 08.925 597 Metres North North East

Agan Ha'ayalot N. 31 51.877 E. 035 08.617 660 Metres South South East

Sde Boaz N. 31 40.924 E. 035 08.764 984 Metres East

Route 1 N. 31 48.806 E. 035 20. 466 253 Metres West South West

Jerusalem Municipal Police Headquarters N. 31 47. 467 E. 035 20.488 North

Pnei Kedem N. 31 35.177 E. 035 11.787 928 Metres East

Kokhav Hashmonaim N.31 57.186 E. 035 21.436 531 Metres North West

Kokhav Hashmonaim N. 31 57.186 E. 035 21.436 531 Metres North

Mitzpe Kramim N. 31. 57.041 E. 035 20.891 614 Metres West

Kokhav Hashmonaim N. 31 57.260 E. 035 20.866 588 Metres East

Shvut Rachel N. 32 03.156 E. 035 18.594 368 Metres East

Nahli'el N. 31 58.448 E. 035 08.077 573 Metres South

Nahli'el N. 31 58.448 E. 035 08.077 573 Metres South

Nahli'el   N. 31 58.448 E. 035 08.077   573 Metres   South

ZEBRA
Men

Nofei Nehemia N. 32 05.929 E. 035 14.124 625 Metres South East

Shdema (dismantled) N. 31 41. 552 E. 035 14. 717 585 Metres North East

Havat Skali N. 32. 09.044 E. 035 22.075 734 Metres South

East Talpiot / Armon HaNatziv   N. 31. 75.391 E. 035 23. 475   West

East Talpiot / Armon HaNatziv N. 31. 75.391 E. 035 23. 475 West

SUPERMAN

Alon Road N. 31 51. 068 E. 035 20.053 386 Metres West

Gilo, view from Har Gilo N. 31. 41. 670 E. 035. 06.720 670 Metres North West

Givat Hamatos N. 31. 44.442 E. 035 12.400 782 Metres West

Givat Hamatos N. 31. 44.328 E. 035 12. 499 801 Metres West

Givat Hamatos N. 31. 44.327 E. 035 12. 510 802 Metres North West

Homesh (dismantled) N. 32 18 29.037 E. 035 11.326 North West

Mount of Olives N. 31 46. 536 E. 035 14. 535 768 Metres North East

Har Homa N. 31 43.137 E. 035. 13. 635 608 Metres South East

Har Homa N. 31 43.137 E. 035. 13. 635 608 Metres South

Har Homa N. 31 43.137 E. 035. 13. 635 608 Metres South West

Har Homa N. 31 43.137 E. 035. 13. 635 608 Metres West

Har Homa N. 31 43.137 E. 035. 13. 635 608 Metres North West

Har Homa N. 31 43.137 E. 035. 13. 635 608 Metres North

Settlement was created under the auspices of a project entitled *This Place*, which invited twelve international photographers to work in residence across Israel and the West Bank. *This Place* consists of a travelling exhibition, companion publications, and a program of live events.

Firstly, I would like to express my gratitude to Frédéric Brenner for inviting me to participate in the project, his help and support cannot be underestimated – thank you. Also many thanks to Matt Brogan who navigated me through numerous logistical problems, and also to the project staff, Hamutal Waisel and Lior Avitan. Production of the family portraits was carried out by Nechama Vairogs and Cheryl Mandel, with additional help from Yosef and Judy Cohen. My photography assistants were Matan Ashkenasy and Avinoam Sternheim, with additional support from Gil Bar, Shmaya Finn and Sarale Gur Lavy. Thanks must go to Charlotte Cotton, Miki Kratsman and Jeff Rosenheim for curatorial oversight. Thank you to Michael Mack, Grégoire Pujade-Lauraine and the staff at MACK. Finally thank you to Molly Murray for text editing.

First edition published by MACK

Design by Nick Waplington and Grégoire Pujade-Lauraine
Printed by optimal media

MACK
mackbooks.co.uk
ISBN 9781907946523

Separation Barrier Factory, Yeroham, Israel N. 30 58. 939 E. 034. 57.078 South West